MILLBROOK ARTS LIBRARY

CRAFTS
FOR
PLAY

edited by
Caroline Bingham
and Karen Foster

The Millbrook Press
Brookfield, Connecticut

Copyright © 1993 Merlion Publishing Ltd
First published in the United States in 1993 by
The Millbrook Press Inc.
2 Old New Milford Road
Brookfield, Connecticut 06804

Contributor: Carole Mahoney
Designers: Jane Brett
          Tracy Carrington
          Roger Fletcher
Cover designer: Tracy Carrington
Picture researcher: Claire Allen
Typesetting coordinator: Gina Brierley

Printed and bound in Great Britain

Library of Congress Cataloging-in-Publication Data

Crafts for play/Caroline Bingham, Karen Foster, editors.
     p. cm. – (Millbrook arts library)
     Includes bibliographical references and index.
     Summary: Introduces the toys, games, and dolls of many cultures and
provides instructions for making some simple toys.
     ISBN 1-56294-096-1 (lib. bdg.)
     1. Toy making – Juvenile literature. [1. Toy making. 2. Handicraft.]
I. Foster, Karen, 1964–   . II. Series.
TT174.C73 1993
745.592–dc20   92-42943
                                                       CIP
                                                        AC

Artwork on pages 24 by Richard Berridge and on pages 14, 25, 33
and 36 by Andrew Midgeley.

Models on pages 29, 31, 32/33 by Jane Brett; pages 13, 23,
24/25 by Tracy Carrington; pages 36/37 by Jasper Diamond and
pages 8/9 by Sybil Gardener.

Photographs on pages 7, 14/15, 17, 18/19, 20, 22, 33, 36/37
and 39 by Roger Fletcher and pages 6/7, 8/9, 10, 12/13, 15, 17,
22/23, 24/25, 29, 31, 32/33, 34/35, 42/43 and 44/45 by
Mike Stannard.

CONTENTS

Ancient toys

This stone fresco from Pompeii shows children at play

Do you have a hobby or pastime which involves making something? Perhaps you enjoy making models from wood or working with wet clay. Woodwork and pottery are both crafts. Craftspeople use their knowledge and skill to transform natural materials into objects with their hands. Many different crafts are practiced throughout the world – jewelry making, weaving, glassblowing and spinning wool are just some of them. Craftspeople make objects that are useful, or beautiful, or both.

And it's not surprising that many of them use their skills to make toys and games. It is much more special to have something carved just for you, than to have a wooden toy made in a factory that is exactly the same as thousands of others! You can tell from looking at this picture from Ancient Rome that children long ago played with toys. Of course, in the past, everything, including toys, had to be made by hand.

A wooden cat from Ancient Egypt

An Iron Age clay cow

Dolls

We can find out about toys in ancient times by looking carefully at paintings, sculptures, carvings, and pottery. They portray children playing with hoops, balls, and dolls. This Roman doll is made from fabric that is very fragile. It is amazing that the doll has survived for 2,000 years in such good condition.

A rag doll from Ancient Rome

Model animals

One of the most popular kind of toy for young children is a model animal. Think of a wooden rocking horse or a furry teddy bear! Model animals were just as popular in ancient times as now. Children in Ancient Egypt, Greece, and Rome played with handcrafted toys modeled in clay, like the Iron Age cow, or carved from wood, like this wild cat. These toys have been found by archaeologists digging on ancient sites. The cat has a moveable jaw with a string to open and close it. It's hard to believe that it is about 3,000 years old!

Making toys

Choosing materials

If you were making a handcrafted toy for yourself or a friend, what materials would you use? If you live in the countryside, you could probably find a piece of wood quite easily from which you could carve an animal or a figure. But what if you live in a city? Perhaps all you could find would be a pile of junk. It wouldn't be easy to make a really good toy from this.

Yet children in many parts of the world where there are few factory-made toys available have always had to use their imagination and ingenuity to make their own toys. Most are vehicles or figures that move on wheels, all sturdily made to be pushed over rough ground. These vehicles from Botswana are made from wire, cloth and string.

Two wire toys
from Botswana

You have seen that ancient toys could be made from wood, clay, and fabric but, in fact, they were made from whatever material was available. It makes sense for craftspeople to use a material they can easily find for their work, so crafted objects often vary from region to region. A pottery bowl from one country might look different to one from another country, because the clay comes from different soil.

Christopher
Dlamini's wire bus

A wire bus

Christopher Dlamini is 10 years old. He lives in a small town called Mbabane in Southern Africa. Christopher made this wire bus. He found some pieces of thick wire that he straightened by stretching them between two heavy stones.

Christopher and his wire bus

He used pliers to cut the wire into the lengths he needed and used the wire to form the framework of the bus. To secure the ends, he joined them together by overlapping them and wrapping thinner wire around the joints.

Christopher shaped many extra features and attached them to the bus in the same way. Look at the features he included – side mirrors, antenna, gear shift, steering wheel, lights, sliding doors, and even a license plate at the front! The wheels are made from soda cans cut in half, with one half pushed into the other to make them strong. No wonder he looked so proud when his photograph was taken.

The simplest toy

Balls from Ancient Egypt

Fabric and leather balls

The brightly colored balls in the picture are made from panels of fabric, stitched together and overlaid with painted reeds. They come from Egypt and probably date back to 1400 BC. The Egyptians also made balls from clay, which was baked hard, then covered with a thin coat of shiny color, or glazed. By the 1400s and 1500s, leather balls were widely found in Europe, where they were used to play a game similar to modern soccer. You can see that the ball had to be filled with air before use.

The simplest toy ever invented is probably a ball. Balls can be formed from so many materials. If you scrunch up a handful of paper and throw it at a friend, you have made a ball! The first balls to be used as toys were probably round fruits or vegetables whose tough skins had been hollowed out and dried. It is likely that balls like these were used only for throwing and catching games because they would not bounce very well. It was not until rubber was used to make balls in the 1800s that they could bounce properly!

A leather ball in use in Italy in the 1600s

Marbles

Marbles, a popular game using miniature balls, has been played since Roman times. Originally, small, round pebbles were rolled in the game, but in the 1700s round chips of marble were introduced into Europe, and the game was given its present name. Today, marbles are made from glass. The first glass marbles were handmade. They were usually clear or white, with streaks of beautiful colors running through them. These handcrafted marbles are now very valuable, and some people will pay a lot of money to have the best marbles in their collections.

A fabric ball

You can make a simple ball from strips of fabric. Make a cardboard shape as shown in the picture, and use it as a guide to cut six fabric strips of the same size. Place the right sides of two strips together, then join them by sewing down one side using a firm running stitch. Repeat, making sure the right sides of your strips are always touching, until you have sewn all the strips together. Now turn the ball inside out. Stuff it with old fabric or newspaper until it is a good sphere shape. Now cut two small circles of fabric and stitch them over the holes at each end. If you have used plain fabric, you could decorate it with felt-tip pens or paints.

Early glass marbles

Carving toys from wood

You can tell by looking at the two animals that the wood-carver who worked them has taken a close look at a real frog and hare. He is aware of how they sit, stand, run, and relax. This observation is a very important part of a wood-carver's craft. The wood-carver has also been careful to show no tool marks.

Two wooden animals

Wood is an ideal material for making into toys because it can be carved to show really tiny details. Carvers make especially good animal toys from wood. The natural color and patterns of wood are just right for showing the polished beak of a duck, the glistening back of a frog, or the shiny fur of a hare.

Carving an animal

Look closely at the wooden frog and hare, pictured on this page. The animals look almost real. The frog is tensed to leap forward. Its legs are drawn back and it is ready to spring. The hare is resting, and has stretched its legs out. How do you think the wood-carver achieved these realistic effects?

He made delicate strokes with a very sharp tool, carefully chipping away the unwanted wood. Then the animals were waxed and polished until the wood shone.

Noah's Ark

Carved wooden toys were very popular in Europe and America during the 1800s. The impressive toy shown at the top of the next page is a Noah's Ark from Germany that was made at this time.

A German Noah's Ark from the 1800s

You may know the religious story of Noah's Ark. It tells how Noah and his family rescued pairs of animals from drowning during a great flood by housing them in a boat called an ark. You can see pairs of giraffes, ostriches, and bears in the picture. How do you think craftspeople of the time made these wooden animals identical, no matter how many arks they made?

Identical animals

They worked out a clever technique, and you may be able to spot how it was done by looking at this picture. First a tree trunk was cut into rings. Each ring was put on a machine called a lathe, which is a machine that spins the wood around, cutting and smoothing it at the same time. The wood-carver then carved one end of the ring into the shape of an animal's legs, body, and head. The lathe then followed the carver's pattern, cutting the whole ring into the shape of that animal. The ring was taken off the lathe and sawn into separate pieces, just like cutting a round cake into slices. Finally, each animal was painted by hand. The wood-carver had made enough pairs of that animal at one time to put into ten or twelve Noah's Arks!

Animals carved from one wooden ring

Wood and string

You have already looked at some wooden toys that take a great deal of skill to make. Some toys and games are easier to make but need a lot of skill to play! They involve the coordination of mind, hand, and eye.

Wheels on a string

Do you recognize the toy shown on this vase from Ancient Greece? If you do, you probably know it as a yo-yo. This is a modern name for a simple toy that was first made thousands of years ago.

The original toy was carved from wood in the shape of two small wheels joined together in the center. String was then wound around the central part. By wrapping the end of the string around one finger and raising the hand up and down, you can make the yo-yo move up and down the string. It can be quite difficult to control! The people of the Philippines must have been able to control them well – in the past, they used a large form of yo-yo as a weapon. They hid in trees, and struck their victims on the head from above!

A detail from an Ancient Greek vase showing a boy playing with a yo-yo

The cup and ball

Cup and ball is a game that sounds simple enough. It's certainly easy to make, as you'll see if you look at the end of the page. A ball, which is tied to a cup with a string, is thrown up and caught in the cup. But the game is more difficult than it sounds. You need to jerk the ball upward with just the right force, or it will go right over the cup. We know that cup and ball was played throughout Europe in the 1500s, 1600s, and 1700s, when it was called bibloquet.

Even kings can be fascinated by children's games! In the late 1500s, Henri III, the King of France, was captivated by the bibloquet. The craze spread from his court and, as you can see from this picture, soon everyone was playing it! The bibloquet was hand-carved from wood and was sometimes painted. Special versions were also made from beautifully carved ivory.

French people playing bibloquet in the 1700s

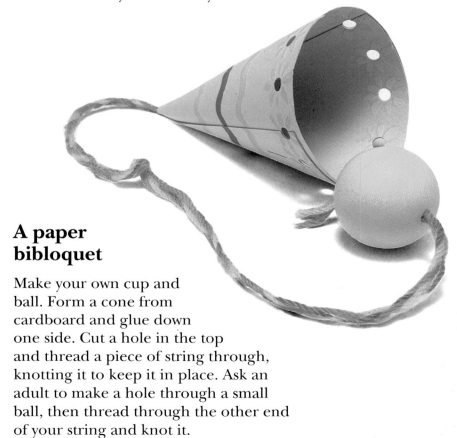

A paper bibloquet

Make your own cup and ball. Form a cone from cardboard and glue down one side. Cut a hole in the top and thread a piece of string through, knotting it to keep it in place. Ask an adult to make a hole through a small ball, then thread through the other end of your string and knot it.

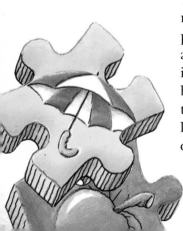

Wooden puzzles

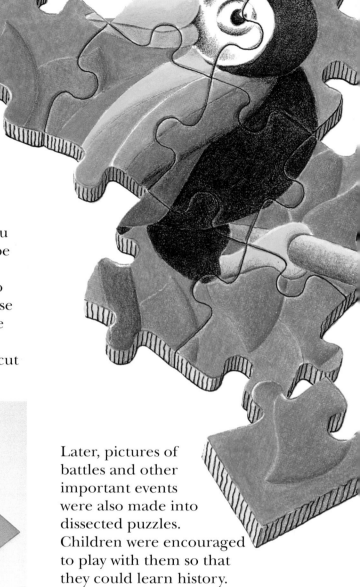

Carved wooden toys like the ones you have already looked at are made to be played with and enjoyed. But some European wooden toys were made to instruct as well as amuse. One of these was the puzzle. The first puzzles were made in the 1760s, and were called dissected puzzles. Dissected means "cut into pieces".

A dissected puzzle made in England in the 1800s

Later, pictures of battles and other important events were also made into dissected puzzles. Children were encouraged to play with them so that they could learn history.

Jigsaw puzzles

You've probably seen wooden puzzles with pictures on them, called jigsaw puzzles. Do you know why we call these

The first puzzles

The first puzzles were made by mapmakers, who stuck beautifully printed maps onto thin mahogany board and then carefully divided the board into pieces by cutting around the borders of each country. As children put the puzzle back together again, they learned about the geography of the countries shown on the map.

These picture bricks from the 1800s show pictures of animals

Wooden picture bricks

games jigsaws? They are named after a machine called a jig saw, which was invented in about 1870. This did the job of cutting wood into complicated shapes more quickly and efficiently than could be done by hand. In fact, jig saws are so efficient that huge puzzles can now be made. The world's largest puzzle can be made in much less time than it would have taken a mapmaker to make a dissected puzzle. It has 61,752 pieces!

Picture bricks are another kind of dissected puzzle. The bricks are cubes with six faces, all the same size. Every cube has one part of a picture on each of its faces. By placing the correct side up and matching the parts of each picture, you can recreate the six whole pictures. Bricks are still popular toys for very young children today, but handmade wooden bricks like the ones in the picture below can be expensive toys.

Dolls from around the world

An African corn-cob doll

Wood, clay, wax, bone, leather, paper, sugar, dough, rags, nuts, wool, corn, straw, potatoes, and apples. You may think that these materials have little in common! But at different times and in different places around the world they have all been used to handcraft dolls.

A corn-cob doll

The corn plant provides some good materials for making homemade dolls. You can see from this picture of an African doll that the corn-cob makes an ideal body. This corn-cob doll has clothes made from fabric and has hair made from wool. But other parts of the corn plant can be used instead. The dried leaves, or husks, make good clothes, and the soft green fibers inside the husks make good hair. So it's not surprising that in almost every part of the world where corn is grown, you can find corn-cob dolls.

Ceremonial dolls

Although the Hopi people of Arizona grow corn, their dolls, called kachinas, are carved out of the wood of a native tree called the cottonwood. The wood is then painted and decorated with leather, feathers, and cloth. Kachina dolls, with their colored costumes and painted bodies, represent Hopi gods and spirits of the earth, sky, sun, wind, and rain. They were given to children after ceremonies and festivals as a way of helping them to learn about the Hopi beliefs.

Apple-head dolls

Early settlers in North America made dolls from apples, called Apple Grannies. You can make your own Apple Granny.

You will need one small, green apple. Peel the apple, then carve out the nose, eyes, and mouth. Mix a spoonful of lemon juice and a spoonful of salt in a small bowl and soak the carved apple in it for 20 minutes to stop the apple from rotting. Take the apple out, pat it dry, then leave it on a wire rack in a place that is dry but not too warm.

Now you will need patience! The apple can take up to three weeks to dry. When you think it is dry enough, stick on two beads for eyes and some cotton wool for hair. To make a simple body, insert a stick into the apple head and cover it with cloth for a dress. You could even make a cap and apron.

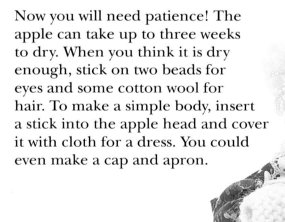

Expensive dolls

Dolls made in Europe during the 1700s and 1800s were so finely crafted that they were very expensive to buy. They were originally made as models to show off the latest fashions. Dressmakers sewed tiny versions of their new fashions, dressed a doll in the clothes, and sent it to customers who could then choose their dresses at home. Dolls like these soon became so popular with the customers' children that they began to be made as toys rather than models.

Porcelain heads

Dolls like the ones in the picture below were made in France in the late 1800s by the firm of Émile Jumeau. The heads of Jumeau dolls were made from a fine clay called porcelain. They were molded in two halves, the back and the front, in plaster casts. These were then baked in a kiln for a day at a very high temperature. When they came out of the kiln, the porcelain had baked to a pure white color, so the pale-pink skin color was painted on.

Four French dolls
from the 1800s

A wax doll made in 1862

Tiny clothes

The finished dolls were then taken to special doll shops to be dressed. Their tiny clothes were handsewn and beautifully trimmed with lace, ribbons, buttons, and jewels by highly skilled dressmakers. They were given hats, shoes, stockings, and gloves – sometimes whole trunks full of extra dresses and accessories.

Dolls' clothes from the 1800s

Modeled in wax

In 1851, a huge exhibition called the Great Exhibition was held in London. Part of the exhibition was a display of the best crafts of the time. A set of dolls made by an English family called Montarari was one part of this display, and it was a huge success at the time. The dolls had heads made from wax. As you can see from the picture, this was a perfect material for a doll's smooth skin.

To make the head, liquid wax was poured into a mold. When it hardened, the wax was smoothed and tinted with color to give it a lifelike appearance. Real hair and eyelashes were then inserted hair by hair into holes made in the hard wax with a hot needle. Glass eyes were added. The dolls had wax limbs and cloth bodies. You can imagine how long one doll took to make!

Wax and porcelain dolls were always expensive to buy in the late 1800s, but they are even more valuable now. Many of them probably survived until today because their owners weren't allowed to play with them very often, in case the dolls were broken. Collectors now pay large amounts of money to own the most beautiful of these old dolls.

Puppets

Puppets are often thought of as dolls that move, but many puppets are not meant to be toys at all. For thousands of years, they have formed an important part of theater in many countries throughout the world. This beautiful puppet is made from decorated leather and comes from Thailand. There, puppet shows are still one of the most popular forms of entertainment. The puppets are controlled by wooden sticks used by a puppeteer who sits behind a screen. Lamps are shone behind the puppets, so that their shadows fall on the screen. The puppets enact religious stories.

A shadow puppet from Thailand

This picture shows a medieval puppet show

Hand puppets

Hand puppets are also made to entertain, but hand-puppet theaters are usually meant for children. This picture shows a European hand-puppet show in the 1300s. Can you see the three young girls who are watching? The puppets were probably made from cloth with carved wooden heads, just as they are today. The puppeteer's fingers control the movements of the puppet's head and arms, but no legs can be seen. The puppeteer remains out of sight.

String puppets

Puppets whose limbs are moved with strings or wires are probably the most popular kind. This is because they are able to make the best movements!

This beautifully decorated string puppet comes from Burma and was made in the 1800s. Its maker has carved and painted its head and limbs, then sewn on the elaborate costume. Many handcrafted string puppets are not as elaborate as this one, but they still make interesting moving toys.

Controlling the strings

Flexible string puppets are sometimes called marionettes. The marionette's strings are fastened to a small wooden frame. The puppeteer is hidden above the stage and operates the puppets by tilting the frame or by moving individual strings with the fingers. Making a puppet move in a realistic way is a highly skilled job! Even the simplest marionettes have nine strings, attached to the ears, shoulders, hands, legs, and one to the back of the puppet. The puppeteer has to concentrate hard to control all these strings at once.

This Burmese puppet was made in the 1800s

Jumping jacks

The toys on this page are controlled by strings, like the puppets you have just read about. The difference is that these figures are flat and only have one master string that jerks them into movement. We call these toys jumping jacks.

A sellout!

This wooden jumping jack comes from France. You can see that it is a simple wood carving, with decorations painted on in bright colors. It probably didn't take a wood-carver very long to make a jumping jack like this. But in France during the 1750s, these moving toys were so popular that people bought them as fast as they were made. Like the craze for playing cup and ball games you

This French jumping jack was made in the 1700s

read about on page 13, both adults and children played with jumping jacks, also called pantins, whenever they could.

Artists began to produce handpainted pantins. They drew the bodies of figures on cards like those on the left, so that people could cut them out and assemble them at home. Eventually, the craze for pantins grew to such an extent that the police ordered craftspeople to stop making them.

The official reason they gave for this ban was that women were in danger of giving birth to children with jerking limbs like pantins! What do you think of this explanation? Historians say that the real reason was that artists had begun to paint pantins that looked like famous people of the time, and that people were using the toys to make fun of them!

Two sheets of hand-drawn pantins from France

Make a jumping jack

It's not against the law to play with jumping jacks now, so why not make one yourself? Choose a character to make. It might be a clown, a dancer, or even one of your friends! Draw the body and head on a piece of cardboard. Draw the arms and legs separately. Color them in, then cut them out. Attach the arms and legs to the body loosely with paper fasteners.

Now use a needle and embroidery thread to loosely join the arms behind the body. Do the same to the legs. Tie a long piece of embroidery thread from the center of the thread joining the arms down to the center of the one joining the legs, leaving a long piece at the bottom to pull. Tie a bead to the end of this thread. Tie a short loop of thread on the jumping jack's head to hang it up. Pull the bead and your jumping jack will come to life!

Windmills

European windmills

Windmills were also popular toys in Europe as long ago as the 1500s. The picture on the opposite page is a detail from a large painting by the Flemish artist Pieter Breughel, called *Children's Games.* Can you see the long wooden sticks the two children in the center are holding? You may think that they look nothing like the paper windmills used in the Springtime Festival in Hong Kong, but this is how early European windmills looked.

Children made square propellers and attached them to the ends of poles. Then, when they pretended to be knights fighting each other with sticks, or lances, the propellers whizzed around as they brandished their poles. Perhaps the sound of the windmill added to the excitement of the game!

Spring is a special time of year in Hong Kong. It is a time when everyone celebrates, with festivals and large picnics outside the city. The children are given elaborate garlands of shiny windmills that glitter as they whir around in the wind. The shops are full of these brightly colored moving toys, but many children still make their own to welcome in the spring, just as their ancestors did hundreds of years before.

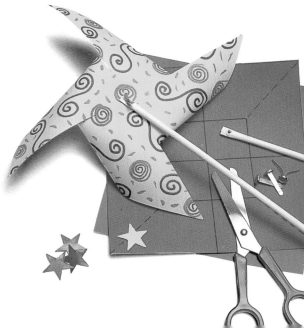

1. Draw two pencil lines as shown

2. Cut along the lines as shown

3. Fasten the corner of each sail in the center as shown

A springtime windmill

Use a square piece of cardboard and a straw to make a springtime windmill. Paint some designs on one side of the cardboard before you start. Now divide the card into four equal triangles with two pencil lines. Mark the point with a dot where the two lines meet. Cut along each of these four lines, making sure you leave a space in the center so that you don't cut the paper into pieces. Now you have the four sails of your windmill.

Fold one corner of each sail into the center, where they should overlap. Pass a metal paper fastener through the overlapping sails and through the dot. Now make a hole in the top of your straw and pass the paper fastener through to the other side. Open the fastener out loosely so that the sails will blow around in the wind.

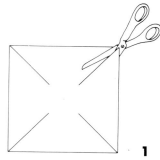

1

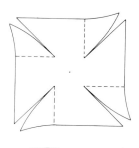

2

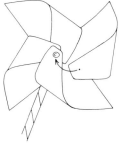

3

Making board games

Can you think why these beautiful glass objects were made? Perhaps they remind you of the pieces used to play a game like checkers. That's certainly what archaeologists thought when they first found the set while excavating an ancient burial mound in England. The pieces are about 3,000 years old and it does seem likely that they were part of a board game, although no one can work out exactly what the rules were!

Glass game pieces from England

Senet

Some very beautiful board games have been found in Ancient Egyptian tombs. In 1922, the archaeologist Howard Carter discovered four examples of the game known as senet among all the other wonderful things in the tomb of the young Egyptian king, Tutankhamen. One of the games is a wooden box like the one shown in this picture. The Egyptian box had a special ebony stand, with legs carved in the shape of a lion's legs with golden paws. The top of the box is the board, with 30 squares inlaid in the wood.

The pieces used to play the game were kept in the drawer. All the Egyptian pieces were missing. Perhaps they were stolen by a tomb robber because they were made from gold or semi-precious stones. Pieces from other senet games have been found made from clay, ivory, and rock crystal.

An ancient senet game

Pachisi

Early travelers visiting the palaces of the emperors of India tell of a board game called pachisi. Sixteen women dressed in red or white were the pieces. The board was marked out in the courtyard of the palace using red and white marble squares, and the players sat on a huge square stone in the middle of the board.

A pachisi game from India

Pachisi is still played in India today. The boards are still very impressive, too – although not on such a large scale! Modern boards are usually made in the shape of a cross, like the one in this picture. They are made from cloth squares embroidered in different colors. Sometimes small, round mirrors are sewn on for decoration. The cone-shaped pieces are carved from wood and painted yellow, black, green, and red. The people who make pachisi boards take great pride in their work, and the best boards are too valuable to play with!

Chess and mancala

Pieces from an Indian chess set

About 1,500 years ago in India, the cross-shaped pachisi board was adapted into a square board, and a new game called chaturanga, or Indian chess, was invented. Chaturanga was a battle game between four armies. Each army had small carved pieces representing foot soldiers, infantry, elephants, and boatmen. The armies were led by a piece representing a prince or king called a rajah. They were finely carved from wood or ivory and painted to look as realistic as possible. The pieces could only move certain ways around the board. The aim of the game was to capture your enemy's army.

From India the game spread around the world, changing as it went. By the time it reached Japan it was very different. Shogi, or Japanese chess, is played on a small table with the top marked as a large rectangle divided into 81 smaller rectangles. Two players each have 20 pieces. The 40 pieces, all the same color, are carved in the shape of small wooden blocks and have their names written on them in Japanese characters.

European chess pieces

These pictures show two chess pieces that were found on an island off the coast of Scotland. They are carved from walrus ivory and are over 800 years old. The figures represent a king and queen. In European chess, the queen leads an army of pieces, including the king, a knight, a bishop, and several soldiers called pawns. Do you think the queen looks happy about being in charge?

Two Isle of Lewis chess pieces

Mancala

There is a game played in Africa where, like chess, the aim is to capture all your opponent's pieces. It is called mancala. In this game, it is the boards rather than the pieces that are carved into an intricate shape. The mancala board in this picture has been made in the shape of a goat.

A goat-shaped mancala board from Africa

You can make your own mancala game from a fruit tray. Cut it so that there are two rows with six holes in each row. Paint your board with bright decorations and varnish it to make it stronger. Start with four small stones or dried beans in each hole, then find a friend to play with you. Here are the rules:

1. The first player takes all four stones from any hole on the right-hand side and puts one into the next four holes, moving in a counter-clockwise direction.

2. When the last of the four stones has been put in a hole, all five stones are picked up from the same hole and the process is repeated.

3. When the last stone falls into an empty hole, the first player's turn is over.

4. The second player takes the stones or stone from any hole on the left side of the board and follows the same process.

5. After this, when any hole contains four stones, the owner of the hole can capture them.

6. If a player gets four stones in a hole with her last stone, she captures them, but her turn finishes. If it happens on her opponent's side, her opponent captures the stones.

7. When only eight stones or less are left on the board, they are taken by the first player and the game is over. Good luck!

Games made from shells

Women Playing the Shell Game was painted by the Japanese artist Kitagawa Utamaro

Have you ever looked closely at clam, mussel, cockle, and oyster shells? They are called bivalves, which means they are formed from two parts. If you have looked at the shells closely, you will see that the two halves are almost identical.

Children in Japan hundreds of years ago played a game in which the pieces were made from bivalve shells. The two parts of each shell were split up and put with others on a flat surface. The aim of the game was to match the two halves together again. The two sides of bivalve shells look so similar that it must have been quite a difficult game to play!

Works of art

Adults in Japan played a similar game called kai-awase. It involved 180 pairs of shells, so it was even more difficult to play. Then the game was developed even further – one side of each pair of shells was painted with identical, jewel-like pictures showing scenes from everyday life in Japan or scenes from nature. They were miniature works of art painted in gold and bright colors. The sets of shells were kept in lacquer boxes, which were themselves beautifully made and painted.

Sometimes parts of poems were written in decorative letters inside the shells, and the players had to recite the beginnings of the poems before they could have another turn. So kai-awase wasn't just a game for fun – it was considered a good way for people to broaden their knowledge and develop a good memory!

Paint your own shells

If you can find some bivalve shells you can make a shell game. You will need 20 pairs of shells of the same kind with their two halves still attached. These may be quite hard to find! Clean them in water, then let them dry.

Before you separate the matching halves, paint the same simple design or write the same letter on both shells of each pair. Varnish the shells so that the designs or letters won't rub off. When the varnish is dry, cut the two halves carefully apart with scissors. Now you are ready to play.

Mix the shells up, then arrange them with the designs facing downward. Put one shell in the middle, then make a circle with 8 shells around it. Now make another circle around that with 13 shells and a final circle with 18 shells. Each player turns over 2 shells. If they match, that player keeps them and has another go. If not, the shells are turned back again and the next player turns over 2 shells. The game soon becomes a test of memory. The winner is the player who matches the most pairs.

Paper toys

The pages of this book are made from paper. You probably use paper to write or draw on every day. But do you ever think about how paper is made? Papermaking is a very ancient craft. It was first practiced nearly 2,000 years ago in China by a man called Ts'ai Lun. An old Chinese history book tells us how he used tree bark, old rags, and fishing nets that he beat to a pulp and then spread out thinly and left in the sun to dry.

This way of making paper was kept a secret by the Chinese for another 600 years, but eventually the secret traveled to Europe. Paper was first made in Spain and Italy, and later in France, Germany, Holland, and England.

Making paper by hand in Korea

It was not long before machines were invented to make all the paper that was needed. But the craft of making fine paper by hand still uses the same method that Ts'ai Lun invented 2,000 years ago. Once the craft of papermaking was established, other crafts developed that used paper to make objects. One of these was the craft of making paper toys. Paper toys are popular because they are cheap and easy to make.

Paper dolls

In India, children play with dolls made from papier mâché. Clay molds of the dolls' arms, legs, and bodies are made first. These are covered with layers of paper stuck together with paste and then left to dry. When dry, they are cut in halves to remove them from the molds, then stuck together again with another layer of paper. The arms and legs are joined to the body with string threaded through at the shoulders and hips. This makes the dolls flexible, so that they can sit or stand. The dolls are painted and dressed in brightly colored paper clothes.

Dancing paper dolls

Try making some simple paper dolls. You will need strong paper, folded as in the first two diagrams. Trace the figure onto the paper and cut away the shaded parts. Unfold the paper and place your four figures as shown. Now cut off the back of the skirts of two opposite figures to make trousers. Finally separate the legs and you have your dancing dolls.

Two Indian paper dolls

1. Fold the paper into eight triangles as shown.

2. Re-do the folds until you have one small triangle.

3. Draw your figure and cut around it as shown.

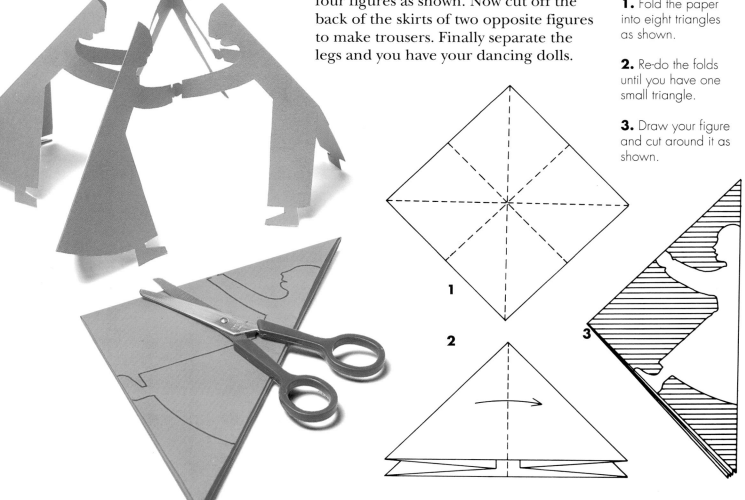

Paper pictures

This English silhouette shows a birthday party

You probably use paper to make pictures quite often. You can paint or draw on it – even stick shapes onto it. But have you ever used scissors to cut a picture out of the paper itself? Cutout paper crafts are popular in many countries.

Paper silhouettes

One kind of cutout paper craft was especially popular in Europe during the 1700s. It was the making of silhouette portraits. In the days before the camera was invented, pictures of people were all painted by artists. This took a long time, a lot of skill, and was very expensive.

A cheaper way of having a portrait done was to have your side view, or profile, cut directly out of a piece of black paper. This craft was named after a French politician called Étienne de Silhouette, whose hobby was making silhouette portraits. He began a fashion for collecting silhouettes that became widespread in the 1800s.

Chinese cutouts

There is a paper craft from China that has its roots in another craft – embroidery. You probably know that the intricate designs of birds and flowers on Chinese embroidery are often repeated many times on one piece of cloth.

Paper decorations

Gradually, another use was found for the cutouts. People found the pictures so beautiful that they began to use them to decorate their houses, especially at holidays, rather than using them as embroidery patterns. The women began to cut the pictures out of red or black paper and stick them onto white paper. This made them stronger so that they would last longer. They were then fastened over windows and the light shone through, showing up all the intricate details. The brightly colored cutouts on these pages are modern examples, made just for decoration.

Chinese paper cutouts

Embroiderers had to make sure that these intricate designs were stitched in exactly the same way each time they were repeated. To make this process easier, they cut their embroidery designs out of very thin paper, then pinned them onto the cloth. The paper patterns could be moved to wherever they were needed on the cloth, and reused.

Paper patterns

Some people became so skilled at making the patterns that they gave up embroidery and concentrated on cutting out the patterns to sell to other embroiderers. The best paper cutters charged high prices for their delicate work.

Origami

The word "origami" is Japanese. In fact it is two Japanese words joined together. "Ori" means to fold and "gami'" means paper. Origami is the craft of folding paper into objects – often animals, flowers, or fish. Although it is called by a Japanese name, nobody knows if the craft originally came from Japan. Some people believe it came from China or Korea. But we do know that it was first developed over 1,000 years ago and that it was practiced at that time in the Imperial Japanese court. The Japanese considered origami to be an elegant and accomplished way to pass the time. Some origami forms are very complicated. They have a special meaning and are used in ceremonies.

Origami models

The skill of folding

Origami is also a form of puzzle solving. It is satisfying to see a piece of paper transformed by just a few folds into a lifelike bird or animal or a beautiful flower or decoration. Traditionally, proper origami paper is used. This is square, colored on one side and white on the other. Sometimes the paper is beautifully decorated. The most important rule of origami is that no cutting or gluing is allowed. The skill lies in making a few single folds. These need to be formed neatly and cleanly by running a thumbnail along each fold to make it sharp. Sometimes several layers of paper are folded at once.

a

d

c

Make an origami penguin

The best way to appreciate the skill demanded by origami is to try it yourself. Follow these instructions to make an origami penguin. First fold your origami square in half to bring **a** and **c** together (**1**). Fold **a** up to form a triangle (**2**). Bring **b** and **d** together, folding the whole shape in half (**3**). Fold back **b** as shown, then **d** (**4**). Fold **b** and **d** forward to form the wings. Bring **c** forward through the body to form the penguin's feet. It will help to note point **e** as the other end of this fold (**5**). Bring **a** forward to form the beak, making a fold at the neck as shown (**6**).

1

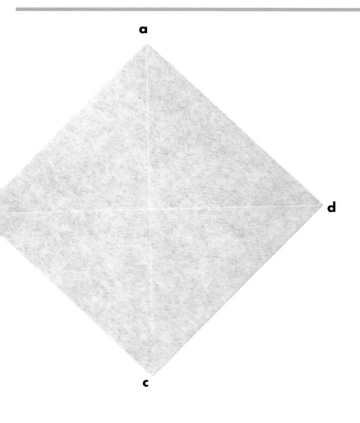

d

ac

2

a

c

3

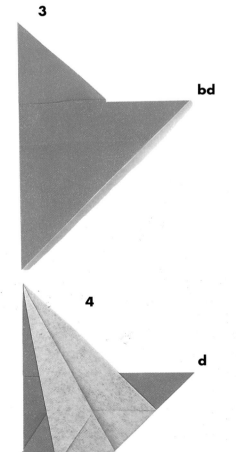

d

bd

4

d

b

c

5

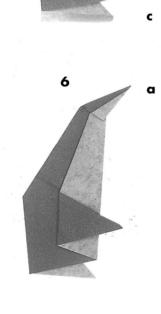

e

bd

c

6

a

Kites

A kite is an object that is flown in the air on the end of a string. Kites made from bamboo frames probably originated in China about 3,000 years ago. These early kites were used in warfare – to measure the distance between one army and the next, or to carry a rope across a dangerous river. Soldiers also tried to scare the enemy by flying musical kites fitted with tightened strings that whistled and wailed in the wind.

Kites being flown at a festival in Japan

This picture of a man flying a kite is from a German manuscript of 1405

Fly a kite

The craft of kite making gradually spread across Asia. It was first recognized as a craft in Europe in the 1400s. As you can see from the picture above, kites at this time looked just like Chinese or Japanese ones. Today, kiteflying is a popular pastime all over the world, and shaped kites are made from many different materials, from paper and plastic to various types of fabric.

Kite festivals

In Japan there is an annual kite-flying festival where competitions involving battles between kites are staged. People stick powdered glass on the string to make it razor sharp. Then they try to cut through an opponent's kite string while the kites are in the air. When a kite falls to the ground, it can be kept by the first person to reach it. Kite festivals are fun to attend and they are beginning to gain in popularity elsewhere.

Chinese kites

In China, the ninth day of the ninth month, September, is a festival called "Climbing the Heights." On this day, everyone goes out to fly beautiful paper kites with wings like fantastic birds, insects, and dragons. Some are so big that a whole team of people is needed to launch and fly them!

Two paper kites from China

If you have a paper kite like the ones on this page, you will need to take care when you are flying it. If the wind is too strong, it can tear the paper. Paper kites are best flown in open spaces with a steady wind. Have fun!

Hand-printed playing cards

If you have a pack of playing cards, look closely at it. You will probably find it has 52 rectangular cards divided into four suits – clubs, diamonds, hearts and spades. Each suit has 10 number cards, ace to 10, and 3 picture or court cards, jack, queen, and king. This kind of pack is probably the most common kind,

but it is not the type that is used throughout the world. Indian playing cards, like the ones in the picture below, are round. The picture cards often represent Vishnu, the Hindu god, and there can be up to 10 suits in all. Indian playing cards can be made from paper, wood, or ivory.

These round playing cards come from India

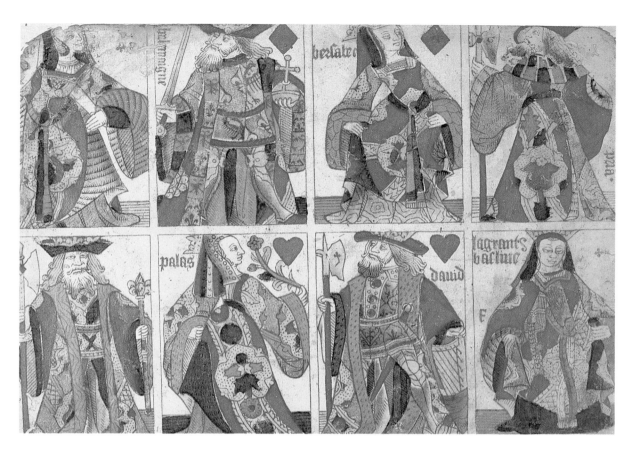

A set of uncut playing cards from the 1800s

Printing the cards

Nobody knows when people first played cards in Europe. We know that playing cards were being used by 1392, because in that year records show that King Charles VI of France paid an artist a great deal of money to paint three packs of cards for him in gold and bright colors.

You probably have a pack of playing cards that was made with thousands of other packs in a factory. The cards shown here from the 1400s and 1600s were hand printed. The design of each card was carved on a wood block. The blocks were placed in a printing press and black ink was rubbed over them. A large sheet of paper was placed under the blocks and the design was printed onto the paper.

Adding color

Colored inks were applied using stencils, one for each color. You can see a sheet of colored prints in the picture above. When the inks were dry, the sheet was pasted onto a thin board and the individual cards were cut out.

Making a wooden carving

Sketching a design onto wood

To begin carving a wooden sculpture, the wood-carver must first have a clear idea of the object he wants to make. Ideas come from looking at the outside world and from the imagination. Sometimes the shape or texture of a particular piece of wood may suggest an idea.

Planning the carving

Once he has chosen his piece of wood, the carver must plan how he will begin to carve. He may make a small model of the finished object in clay or he may sketch a design onto the wood. The carver must be very confident to work directly on the wood.

Roughing out

Now the woodworker can start to carve. He begins by using a saw to remove large pieces of wood. Then he uses different-shaped gouges to make the round and hollow shapes required. They are tapped with a mallet. The gouge must be very sharp and care must be taken. Wood cannot be put back once it has been removed. The wood-carver works slowly all around the wood to create the rough shape of the sculpture.

The shape emerges

Gradually, the form of the object becomes clearer. The carver now has to decide what detail to add or whether to leave the sculpture simple. He may want to leave the marks of the tools on the wood. Or he may create the detail with a chisel and then smooth the surface with sandpaper. Sometimes he paints on a dye to color the wood at this stage.

Finishing off

Finally, the carver coats the sculpture with oil. When this has dried, the surface is waxed to bring out the patterns and color of the wood. The carving is finished.

1. The wood-carver sharpens a gouge

2. He gouges away wood to create the rough shape of the object

3. The fine details have been made with a chisel

4. The sculpture is coated with oil

Crafts on display

The interior of Pollock's Toy Museum in London

This book has shown you a selection of craft objects from different countries and different times in history. Of course, there are thousands more objects that are just as beautiful and unusual! A good way to see interesting craft objects for yourself is to visit a museum or gallery. Museums collect and exhibit all sorts of different objects, many of them handmade hundreds of years ago, and you can spend as long as you like looking at their collections.

Which museum?

Museums vary greatly. If you live in a large city, you may have the choice of several museums to visit. Some of them may specialize in exhibiting objects of a particular kind like clay or textiles. These museums may have extremely old or rare objects – perhaps even objects that are famous throughout the world.

If you live in a smaller town, there may be a local museum you can visit. It is more likely that smaller museums will contain all kinds of exhibits and that the

craft objects will be mixed with other kinds of objects. But that may make your day even more interesting. And the picture above shows you that a small museum can still be packed full of objects.

Learning as you look

Most museums have good systems for labeling each object so that you can learn how old the object is, where it comes from and something about it as you look. Many museums have specially written catalogs that will give you even more information. And don't forget about the people who work in the museum. There's usually someone who will be pleased to answer your questions. The museums may offer talks or guided tours, specially geared to children or adults, in which you can learn much more about particular exhibits. So enjoy a visit to a museum – and learn more about craft at the same time.

Start a collection!

Obviously you cannot collect the objects that you see in a museum, but if you see something that you find particularly interesting, visit the museum shop and see if they have a picture postcard on sale. Each time you visit a museum or gallery, add to your postcard collection. Try to collect postcards of similar objects made at different times and in different countries, so that you can begin to see how techniques change and how a country's culture affects design.

This picture shows craft objects on display at the British Museum in London

Index

Acknowledgments

The publishers would like to thank the following for permission to reproduce these photographs:

The Ancient Art and Architecture Collection for stone fresco from Pompeii (page 4). Bildarchiv Preussicher Kulturbesitz, Berlin for Ancient Greek vase (page 12). The Bodleian Library, Oxford for medieval puppet show (page 20). The Bridgeman Art Library for *Children's Games* by Pieter Breughel the Elder (page 25); uncut playing cards (page 41) and hand-colored playing cards (page 41). The Trustees of the British Museum for cat (page 5); Ancient Roman rag doll (page 5); clay cow (page 5); Ancient Egyptian balls (page 8); glass game pieces (page 26); senet board (page 26); Isle of Lewis chess pieces (page 28) and *Women Playing the Shell Game* by Kitagawa Utamaro (page 30). Christie's for four porcelain-head dolls (page 18); Indian chess set (page 28). Collections/Geoff Howard for inside the British Museum (page 44). Michael Holford for African corn cob doll (page 16) and wax doll (page 19). The Horniman Museum and Gardens for spruce ring animals (page 11); pachisi game (page 27) and Indian playing cards (page 40). The Hulton Picture Library for early Italian football game (page 8) and French people playing cup and ball (page 13). Hutchison Library for making paper in Korea (page 32). Carole Mahoney for Christopher Dlamini and his wire bus (page 7); Hopi doll (page 17); apple-head doll (page 17); Indonesian shadow puppet (page 20) and Mexican paper dolls (page 33). S&O Mathews for marbles (pages 8/9). Museum fur Volkerkunde for African mancala board (page 29). Niedersächsische Staats-und Universitätsbibliothek, Göttingen for medieval kite flyer (page 38). Picturepoint for Japanese kites (page 38). Pollock's Toy Museum for dissected puzzle (page 14); picture bricks (page 15); dolls' clothes (page 19) and French pantin (page 22). The Board of Trustees of the Victoria and Albert Museum for Noah's Ark (page 11); Burmese string puppet (page 21) and Victorian silhouette (page 34).

The publishers would also like to give special thanks to Carole Mahoney for the loan of items for photography and to Michael Henderson for advice and for allowing himself to be photographed for the book.